A Taste Of Italy

Mastering the Art of Italian Cuisine

Copyright-All Rights Reserved

This book has copyright protection. You can use the book for personal purpose. You should not see, use, alter, distribute, quote, take excerpts or paraphrase in part or whole the material contained in this book without obtaining the permission of the author first.

Table Of Contents

Introduction 1

Chapter 1: Pasta and Risotto 3

Chapter 2: Soups And Salads 15

Chapter 3: Vegetarian Sides
And Mains 36

Chapter 4: Poultry And Meat 43
Mains

Chapter 5: Pizza 52

Chapter 6: Seafood Mains 59

Thank you 70

Introduction

Welcome to "A Taste of Italy," a culinary journey that will transport you to the charming landscapes, rich traditions, and exquisite flavors of one of the world's most beloved cuisines. In the pages of this cookbook, we invite you to embark on a delicious adventure through the diverse regions of Italy, where each dish tells a story and every bite is a celebration of life, family, and the joy of eating.

Italy is a land where food is more than sustenance; it is an expression of love, a connection to the past, and a source of boundless inspiration. From the bustling markets of Rome to the sun-soaked vineyards of Tuscany, and the enchanting coasts of the Amalfi, every corner of Italy has its own unique culinary treasures waiting to be uncovered.

In "A Taste of Italy," we've curated a collection of timeless recipes that pay homage to the heart and soul of Italian cooking. Whether you're a seasoned home cook or a novice in the kitchen, these recipes are designed to transport you to the heart of Italy, allowing you to create authentic and unforgettable dishes right in your own home.

But "A Taste of Italy" is not just about recipes; it's about embracing the Italian philosophy of savoring life's pleasures. It's about gathering around the table with friends and family, sharing stories, laughter, and the sheer delight of a well-prepared meal. It's about taking the time to appreciate the beauty in a ripe tomato, the aroma of freshly baked focaccia, and the satisfaction of crafting a meal from scratch.

We invite you to immerse yourself in the world of "A Taste of Italy." Let these recipes guide you on a culinary voyage that transcends borders and connects you to the very essence of Italian culture. May these dishes become a part of your own family traditions, and may each bite fill your senses with the warmth and magic of Italy.

Buon appetito!

Spaghetti "Aglio E Olio"

"Spaghetti Aglio e Olio" is a classic Italian pasta dish known for its simplicity and incredible flavors. Here's the recipe:

Ingredients:

12 ounces (340g) spaghetti
1/2 cup extra-virgin olive oil
6-8 garlic cloves, thinly sliced
1/2 teaspoon red pepper flakes (adjust to your preferred level of spiciness)
1/4 cup fresh parsley, chopped
Salt, to taste
Grated Parmesan cheese (optional, for serving)

Instructions:

Cook the spaghetti in a large pot of boiling salted water until al dente. Follow the package instructions for cooking time. Reserve about 1 cup of the pasta cooking water before draining the spaghetti.
While the spaghetti cooks, heat the olive oil in a large skillet over medium heat. Add the sliced garlic and red pepper flakes. Cook, stirring occasionally, until the garlic turns golden and aromatic. Be careful not to burn the garlic, as it can become bitter.
Once the spaghetti is cooked, transfer it directly to the skillet with the garlic-infused oil. Toss the spaghetti to coat it evenly with the oil and garlic mixture. If the pasta seems too dry, add some of the reserved pasta cooking water a little at a time until you reach your desired consistency.
Sprinkle chopped parsley over the spaghetti and toss again to distribute it throughout the pasta.
Season the Spaghetti Aglio e Olio with salt to taste. Be mindful of the salt, as the pasta cooking water and Parmesan cheese (if using) also contribute to the overall saltiness.
Optional: Serve the Spaghetti Aglio e Olio with grated Parmesan cheese on top for an extra layer of flavor.
Enjoy this classic Italian dish "Spaghetti Aglio e Olio" as a simple and satisfying meal. The combination of garlic-infused olive oil, red pepper flakes, and fresh parsley creates a delightful medley of flavors. This recipe is perfect for a quick weeknight dinner or a special occasion, as it comes together in no time and never fails to impress with its delicious simplicity. Buon appetito!

Pasta Napoletana

"Pasta Napoletana" is a classic Italian pasta dish that hails from Naples, the birthplace of pizza and many other delicious Italian dishes. This recipe features a flavorful tomato-based sauce that is both simple and delicious. Here's how to make it:

Ingredients:

- 12 ounces (340g) pasta of your choice (spaghetti, penne, or rigatoni work well)
- 2 tablespoons olive oil
- 1 small onion, finely chopped
- 2 garlic cloves, minced
- 1 can (28 ounces) crushed tomatoes
- 1 teaspoon dried oregano
- 1 teaspoon dried basil
- 1/2 teaspoon red pepper flakes (optional, for a hint of spiciness)
- Salt and black pepper, to taste
- Fresh basil leaves, torn, for garnish
- Grated Parmesan cheese, for serving

Instructions:

Cook the pasta in a large pot of boiling salted water until al dente. Follow the package instructions for cooking time. Reserve about 1 cup of the pasta cooking water before draining the pasta.

While the pasta cooks, heat the olive oil in a large skillet over medium heat. Add the chopped onion and sauté until it becomes translucent and slightly golden.

Stir in the minced garlic and cook for another minute until fragrant.

Pour in the crushed tomatoes, dried oregano, dried basil, and red pepper flakes (if using). Season with salt and black pepper to taste. Stir everything together and let the sauce simmer for about 10-15 minutes, allowing the flavors to meld and the sauce to thicken.

Once the pasta is cooked, add it directly to the skillet with the Napoletana sauce. Toss the pasta gently to coat it evenly with the sauce. If the sauce seems too thick, add some of the reserved pasta cooking water a little at a time until you reach your desired consistency.

Serve the Pasta Napoletana in individual plates or a large serving dish. Garnish with torn fresh basil leaves and sprinkle some grated Parmesan cheese on top, if desired.

Enjoy this traditional Italian pasta dish "Pasta Napoletana" with its rich tomato sauce and aromatic herbs. It's a comforting and satisfying meal that will transport your taste buds straight to the heart of Italy. Buon appetito!

Penne With Pesto

Penne with Pesto is a delightful and vibrant Italian pasta dish that brings together the fresh flavors of basil, garlic, pine nuts, and Parmesan cheese. Here's how to make this classic recipe:

Ingredients:

12 ounces (340g) penne pasta
2 cups fresh basil leaves
1/3 cup pine nuts (you can also use walnuts or almonds)
2-3 garlic cloves, peeled
1/2 cup grated Parmesan cheese
1/2 cup extra-virgin olive oil
Salt and black pepper, to taste
Optional: a squeeze of fresh lemon juice

Instructions:

Cook the penne pasta in a large pot of boiling salted water until al dente. Follow the package instructions for cooking time. Reserve about 1 cup of the pasta cooking water before draining the pasta.
While the pasta cooks, prepare the pesto sauce. In a food processor or blender, combine the fresh basil leaves, pine nuts, garlic cloves, and grated Parmesan cheese.
With the food processor or blender running, slowly drizzle in the extra-virgin olive oil until the mixture forms a smooth and creamy sauce. If the pesto is too thick, you can add a little more olive oil to reach your desired consistency.
Season the pesto sauce with salt and black pepper to taste. For an extra burst of freshness, you can also add a squeeze of fresh lemon juice.
Once the penne is cooked, drain it and return it to the pot. Add the prepared pesto sauce to the penne and toss gently to coat the pasta evenly with the flavorful sauce. If the pasta seems too dry, add some of the reserved pasta cooking water a little at a time until you reach your desired sauciness.
Serve the Penne with Pesto in individual plates or a large serving dish. Garnish with a few extra basil leaves or some extra grated Parmesan cheese, if desired.
Enjoy this delicious Penne with Pesto as a vibrant and refreshing pasta dish that celebrates the essence of Italian cuisine. The aromatic basil and nutty pesto sauce perfectly complement the penne, creating a delightful harmony of flavors. It's a quick and easy recipe that's sure to become a favorite at your table. Buon appetito!

Spaghetti With Marinara Sauce

Ingredients:

12 ounces (340g) spaghetti
2 tablespoons olive oil
1 small onion, finely chopped
2 garlic cloves, minced
1 can (28 ounces) crushed tomatoes
1 teaspoon dried oregano
1 teaspoon dried basil
1/2 teaspoon sugar (optional, to balance acidity)
Salt and black pepper, to taste
Fresh basil leaves, torn, for garnish
Grated Parmesan cheese, for serving

Instructions:

Cook the spaghetti in a large pot of boiling salted water until al dente. Follow the package instructions for cooking time. Reserve about 2 cup of the pasta cooking water before draining the spaghetti.
While the spaghetti cooks, heat the olive oil in a large skillet over medium heat. Add the chopped onion and saute until it becomes translucent and slightly golden.
Stir in the minced garlic and cook for another minute until fragrant.
Pour in the crushed tomatoes, dried oregano, dried basil, and sugar (if using). Season with salt and black pepper to taste. Stir everything together and let the sauce simmer for about 10-15 minutes, allowing the flavors to meld and the sauce to thicken.
Once the spaghetti is cooked, add it directly to the skillet with the Marinara sauce. Toss the spaghetti gently to coat it evenly with the sauce. If the sauce seems too thick, add some of the reserved pasta cooking water a little at a time until you reach your desired consistency.
Serve the Spaghetti with Marinara Sauce in individual plates or a large serving dish. Garnish with torn fresh basil leaves and sprinkle some grated Parmesan cheese on top, if desired.

Pasta With Walnut Sauce

Pasta with Walnut Sauce is a delicious and unique Italian pasta dish that features a creamy and nutty sauce made with walnuts, garlic, and Parmesan cheese. Here's how to make this delightful recipe:

Ingredients:

12 ounces (340g) pasta of your choice (linguine or fettuccine work well)
1 cup walnuts, toasted
2 garlic cloves, peeled
1/2 cup grated Parmesan cheese
1/2 cup extra-virgin olive oil
1/2 cup fresh parsley, chopped (optional, for garnish)
Salt and black pepper, to taste

Instructions:

Cook the pasta in a large pot of boiling salted water until al dente. Follow the package instructions for cooking time. Reserve about 1 cup of the pasta cooking water before draining the pasta.

While the pasta cooks, toast the walnuts in a dry skillet over medium heat until they become fragrant and slightly browned. Be careful not to burn them. Once toasted, set aside a handful of walnuts for garnish.

In a food processor or blender, combine the toasted walnuts, garlic cloves, and grated Parmesan cheese. Pulse until the mixture becomes a coarse paste.

With the food processor or blender running, slowly drizzle in the extra-virgin olive oil until the sauce becomes smooth and creamy. You may need to scrape down the sides of the processor or blender to ensure everything is well combined.

Season the walnut sauce with salt and black pepper to taste.

Once the pasta is cooked, drain it and return it to the pot. Add the walnut sauce to the pasta and toss gently to coat the pasta evenly with the creamy sauce. If the sauce seems too thick, add some of the reserved pasta cooking water a little at a time until you reach your desired consistency.

Optional: Garnish the Pasta with Walnut Sauce with the reserved toasted walnuts and chopped fresh parsley for added texture and flavor.

Enjoy this unique and flavorful Pasta with Walnut Sauce as a delightful change from traditional pasta dishes. The combination of creamy walnut sauce, nutty Parmesan, and garlic creates a satisfying and comforting meal. It's a recipe that will impress your guests and leave them craving more. Buon appetito!

Spaghetti Carbonara

Spaghetti Carbonara is a classic Italian pasta dish known for its creamy and rich sauce made with eggs, cheese, pancetta (or guanciale), and black pepper. Here's how to make this delicious and indulgent recipe:

Ingredients:

12 ounces (340g) spaghetti
4 large eggs
1 cup grated Pecorino Romano cheese (or Parmesan)
4 ounces (113g) pancetta or guanciale, diced (you can also use bacon as a substitute)
2 garlic cloves, minced
Freshly ground black pepper, to taste
Salt, if needed (be cautious with salt as the pancetta and cheese are already salty)
Fresh parsley, chopped, for garnish (optional)

Instructions:

Cook the spaghetti in a large pot of boiling salted water until al dente. Follow the package instructions for cooking time. Reserve about 1 cup of the pasta cooking water before draining the spaghetti.

In a bowl, whisk together the eggs and grated Pecorino Romano cheese until well combined. Season with a generous amount of freshly ground black pepper. Set the mixture aside.

In a large skillet, cook the diced pancetta (or guanciale) over medium heat until it becomes crispy and golden. Remove some of the rendered fat from the skillet, leaving about 2 tablespoons to use in the sauce.

Reduce the heat to low, and add the minced garlic to the skillet with the pancetta. Cook for about a minute until the garlic becomes fragrant, being careful not to burn it.

Once the spaghetti is cooked, immediately transfer it to the skillet with the pancetta and garlic, tossing to coat the pasta with the rendered fat and flavors.

Off the heat, pour the egg and cheese mixture over the spaghetti, tossing quickly and continuously to create a creamy sauce. The residual heat from the pasta will cook the eggs, creating a luscious and velvety carbonara sauce. If the sauce seems too thick, add some of the reserved pasta cooking water a little at a time until you reach your desired consistency.

Season the Spaghetti Carbonara with black pepper to taste. Be cautious with salt, as the pancetta and cheese are already salty.

Optional: Garnish the Spaghetti Carbonara with chopped fresh parsley for a burst of color and added freshness.

Pasta With Sun Dried Tomato Pesto

Pasta with Sun-Dried Tomato Pesto is a flavorful and vibrant Italian pasta dish that showcases the intense flavors of sun-dried tomatoes, garlic, basil, and Parmesan cheese. It's a quick and easy recipe that's perfect for a satisfying weeknight dinner. Here's how to make it:

Ingredients:

12 ounces (340g) pasta of your choice (penne, fusilli, or farfalle work well)
1 cup sun-dried tomatoes (dry-packed or in oil), drained if in oil
2 garlic cloves
1/3 cup pine nuts (you can also use almonds or walnuts)
1/2 cup grated Parmesan cheese
1/2 cup fresh basil leaves
1/3 cup extra-virgin olive oil
Salt and black pepper, to taste
Optional: Red pepper flakes for a hint of spiciness
Grated Parmesan cheese and fresh basil leaves, for garnish

Instructions:

Cook the pasta in a large pot of boiling salted water until al dente. Follow the package instructions for cooking time. Reserve about 1 cup of the pasta cooking water before draining the pasta.

While the pasta cooks, prepare the sun-dried tomato pesto. In a food processor or blender, combine the sun-dried tomatoes, garlic cloves, pine nuts, grated Parmesan cheese, and fresh basil leaves.

Pulse the ingredients until they form a coarse paste. While the food processor or blender is running, slowly drizzle in the extra-virgin olive oil until the mixture becomes a smooth and creamy pesto sauce.

Season the sun-dried tomato pesto with salt and black pepper to taste. If you prefer some heat, you can also add red pepper flakes.

Once the pasta is cooked, drain it and return it to the pot. Add the sun-dried tomato pesto to the pasta and toss gently to coat the pasta evenly with the flavorful sauce. If the sauce seems too thick, add some of the reserved pasta cooking water a little at a time until you reach your desired consistency.

Serve the Pasta with Sun-Dried Tomato Pesto in individual plates or a large serving dish. Garnish with grated Parmesan cheese and fresh basil leaves for added texture and flavor.

Spaghetti Puttanesca

Spaghetti Puttanesca is a classic Italian pasta dish known for its bold and robust flavors. The sauce is made with tomatoes, olives, capers, anchovies, garlic, and red pepper flakes, creating a zesty and savory combination. Here's how to make this delicious and aromatic recipe:

Ingredients:
12 ounces (340g) spaghetti
2 tablespoons olive oil
4-6 anchovy fillets (optional, but traditional)
3 garlic cloves, minced
1 can (28 ounces) crushed tomatoes
1/2 cup pitted black olives, sliced
2 tablespoons capers, rinsed and drained
1/2 teaspoon red pepper flakes (adjust to your spice preference)
Salt and black pepper, to taste
Fresh parsley, chopped, for garnish (optional)

Instructions:
Cook the spaghetti in a large pot of boiling salted water until al dente. Follow the package instructions for cooking time. Reserve about 1 cup of the pasta cooking water before draining the spaghetti.
While the pasta cooks, heat the olive oil in a large skillet over medium heat. If using anchovy fillets, add them to the skillet and cook for a minute or two until they dissolve into the oil.
Stir in the minced garlic and cook for another minute until fragrant.
Add the crushed tomatoes to the skillet, along with the sliced black olives, capers, and red pepper flakes. Season with black pepper (and salt, if needed, keeping in mind that the anchovies and capers are already salty). Let the sauce simmer for about 10-15 minutes, allowing the flavors to meld and the sauce to thicken slightly.
Once the spaghetti is cooked, drain it and return it to the pot. Add the Puttanesca sauce to the spaghetti and toss gently to coat the pasta evenly with the zesty and savory sauce. If the sauce seems too thick, add some of the reserved pasta cooking water a little at a time until you reach your desired consistency.
Serve the Spaghetti Puttanesca in individual plates or a large serving dish. Garnish with chopped fresh parsley for a burst of color and added freshness.
Enjoy this Spaghetti Puttanesca as a vibrant and flavorful pasta dish that celebrates the boldness of Italian cuisine. The combination of tomatoes, olives, capers, and anchovies creates a taste experience that's both tangy and satisfying. It's a quick and easy recipe that's perfect for a memorable dinner with family and friends.
Buon appetito!

Fettuccine Alfredo

Fettuccine Alfredo is a classic Italian pasta dish known for its creamy and indulgent sauce made with butter, Parmesan cheese, and heavy cream. It's a simple yet decadent recipe that's sure to please your taste buds. Here's how to make this rich and comforting dish:

Ingredients:

12 ounces (340g) fettuccine pasta
1/2 cup unsalted butter
1 cup heavy cream
1 cup grated Parmesan cheese
Salt and black pepper, to taste
Fresh parsley, chopped, for garnish (optional)

Instructions:

Cook the fettuccine pasta in a large pot of boiling salted water until al dente. Follow the package instructions for cooking time. Reserve about 1 cup of the pasta cooking water before draining the fettuccine.

While the pasta cooks, prepare the Alfredo sauce. In a large skillet over medium heat, melt the unsalted butter. Once the butter is melted, add the heavy cream to the skillet and stir to combine.

Bring the cream and butter mixture to a gentle simmer, stirring frequently to prevent scorching.

Gradually whisk in the grated Parmesan cheese, a little at a time, until it fully melts into the sauce and becomes smooth and creamy. Continue to stir the sauce until it thickens slightly, about 2-3 minutes.

Season the Alfredo sauce with salt and black pepper to taste. Be cautious with salt, as the Parmesan cheese is already salty.

Once the fettuccine is cooked, drain it and return it to the pot. Add the Alfredo sauce to the fettuccine and toss gently to coat the pasta evenly with the luxurious and velvety sauce. If the sauce seems too thick, add some of the reserved pasta cooking water a little at a time until you reach your desired consistency.

Serve the Fettuccine Alfredo in individual plates or a large serving dish. Garnish with chopped fresh parsley for a pop of color and added freshness.

Enjoy this Fettuccine Alfredo as a delightful and indulgent pasta dish that's perfect for special occasions or when you want to treat yourself to a comforting meal. The rich and creamy sauce combined with the silky fettuccine noodles creates a luxurious taste experience that's truly unforgettable. Buon appetito!

Risotto with garlic and chilli

Risotto with Garlic and Chili is a flavorful and aromatic Italian dish that combines the creaminess of risotto with the bold flavors of garlic and chili. The result is a comforting and spicy risotto that's perfect as a side dish or a main course. Here's how to make this delicious recipe:

Ingredients:

1 ½ cups Arborio rice (risotto rice)

4 cups vegetable or chicken broth (low-sodium, if possible)

2 tablespoons olive oil

4 cloves garlic, minced

1 small red chili pepper, finely chopped (adjust amount according to your spice preference)

½ cup dry white wine (optional)

½ cup grated Parmesan cheese

2 tablespoons unsalted butter

Salt and black pepper, to taste

Fresh parsley, chopped, for garnish (optional)

Instructions:

In a medium saucepan, heat the vegetable or chicken broth over low heat. Keep it warm throughout the cooking process.

In a large skillet or saucepan, heat the olive oil over medium heat. Add the minced garlic and chopped chili pepper. Sauté for about a minute until the garlic becomes fragrant and the chili pepper releases its aroma.

Add the Arborio rice to the skillet and stir to coat the rice with the oil, garlic, and chili mixture. Toast the rice for a minute or two until it becomes slightly translucent.

Optional: Pour in the dry white wine and stir until the liquid is mostly absorbed by the rice.

Begin adding the warm broth to the rice, one ladleful at a time. Stir the rice frequently and allow the liquid to be absorbed before adding the next ladleful. Continue this process, stirring often, until the rice is creamy and cooked to your desired level of tenderness. It should take about 18-20 minutes.

Once the risotto is cooked to your liking, stir in the grated Parmesan cheese and unsalted butter. Season with salt and black pepper to taste. The butter and cheese will add creaminess and richness to the risotto.

Serve the Risotto with Garlic and Chili in individual plates or a large serving dish. Garnish with chopped fresh parsley for added freshness and a pop of color.

Risotto alla Certosina

Risotto alla Certosina is a delicious and traditional Italian risotto recipe that originates from the Certosa di Pavia, a historic monastery near Milan. This risotto is known for its rich and flavorful combination of saffron, butter, Parmesan cheese, and bone marrow. The bone marrow adds a unique depth of flavor and richness to the dish. Here's how to make this special Risotto alla Certosina:

Ingredients:
1 ½ cups Arborio rice (risotto rice)
4 cups chicken or vegetable broth (low-sodium, if possible)
1 small onion, finely chopped
2 tablespoons unsalted butter
2 tablespoons olive oil
1/4 cup dry white wine (optional)
A pinch of saffron threads
2 tablespoons hot water
2-3 pieces of bone marrow (about 2 inches each)
1/2 cup grated Parmesan cheese
Salt and black pepper, to taste
Fresh parsley, chopped, for garnish (optional)

Instructions:

In a small bowl, soak the saffron threads in the hot water and set it aside to infuse.
In a medium saucepan, heat the chicken or vegetable broth over low heat. Keep it warm throughout the cooking process.
In a large skillet or saucepan, heat the olive oil and 1 tablespoon of butter over medium heat. Add the finely chopped onion and sauté until it becomes translucent and soft.
Add the Arborio rice to the skillet and stir to coat the rice with the oil and onions. Toast the rice for a minute or two until it becomes slightly translucent.
Optional: Pour in the dry white wine and stir until the liquid is mostly absorbed by the rice.
Begin adding the warm broth to the rice, one ladleful at a time. Stir the rice frequently and allow the liquid to be absorbed before adding the next ladleful. Continue this process, stirring often, until the rice is creamy and cooked to your desired level of tenderness. It should take about 18-20 minutes.
While the risotto is cooking, prepare the bone marrow. In a separate skillet, melt the remaining tablespoon of butter over medium heat. Add the bone marrow pieces and cook them until they become soft and begin to release their rich flavors.
Once the risotto is cooked to your liking, stir in the infused saffron water, grated Parmesan cheese, and the cooked bone marrow. Season with salt and black pepper to taste.
Serve the Risotto alla Certosina in individual plates or a large serving dish. Garnish with chopped fresh parsley for added freshness and a pop of color.

Soups And Salads

Italian Wedding Soup

Italian Wedding Soup is a hearty and comforting soup that features flavorful meatballs, vegetables, and pasta in a delicious broth. Despite its name, the soup is not typically served at Italian weddings but is believed to be named "wedding soup" due to the perfect marriage of flavors. Here's how to make this classic Italian dish:

Ingredients for Meatballs:

- 1/2 pound ground beef
- 1/2 pound ground pork
- 1/4 cup breadcrumbs
- 1/4 cup grated Parmesan cheese
- 1/4 cup chopped fresh parsley
- 1 egg
- 2 cloves garlic, minced
- 1/4 teaspoon dried oregano
- Salt and black pepper, to taste

Ingredients for Soup:

- 6 cups chicken broth (low-sodium, if possible)
- 1 cup small pasta (such as acini di pepe, orzo, or small shells)
- 2 cups fresh spinach, chopped
- 1 carrot, diced
- 1 celery stalk, diced
- 1 small onion, finely chopped
- 2 tablespoons olive oil
- 1/4 cup grated Parmesan cheese (for serving)
- Fresh basil leaves, chopped (for garnish)

Instructions:

To make the meatballs, in a large mixing bowl, combine the ground beef, ground pork, breadcrumbs, grated Parmesan cheese, chopped parsley, minced garlic, dried oregano, egg, salt, and black pepper. Mix everything together until well combined.

Roll the mixture into small meatballs, about 1 inch in diameter. Place the meatballs on a plate or tray and set aside.

In a large soup pot, heat the olive oil over medium heat. Add the chopped onion, diced carrot, and diced celery. Sauté for a few minutes until the vegetables become tender and the onion turns translucent.

Pour the chicken broth into the pot and bring it to a simmer. Add the meatballs to the simmering broth and cook for about 10 minutes, until the meatballs are cooked through.

Stir in the small pasta and cook for an additional 5-7 minutes until the pasta is al dente.

Add the chopped fresh spinach to the soup and cook for a couple of minutes until it wilts. Season the soup with additional salt and black pepper, to taste.

Ladle the Italian Wedding Soup into serving bowls. Sprinkle grated Parmesan cheese over each serving and garnish with chopped fresh basil leaves.

Enjoy this Italian Wedding Soup as a comforting and flavorful dish that brings together the perfect combination of tender meatballs, vegetables, pasta, and a delicious broth. It's a delightful soup that's sure to warm your heart and please your taste buds. Buon appetito!

Chicken Gnocchi Soup

Chicken Gnocchi Soup is a creamy and comforting soup that features tender pieces of chicken, pillowy gnocchi, and vegetables in a rich and flavorful broth. It's a delicious and satisfying dish that's perfect for colder days or when you're in the mood for a hearty and comforting meal. Here's how to make this delightful soup:

Ingredients:

1 tablespoon olive oil
1 tablespoon unsalted butter
1 small onion, finely chopped
2 carrots, diced
2 celery stalks, diced
3 cloves garlic, minced
1 pound boneless, skinless chicken breasts or thighs, cooked and shredded
4 cups chicken broth (low-sodium, if possible)
2 cups half-and-half or heavy cream
1 package (16 ounces) store-bought or homemade gnocchi
2 cups fresh baby spinach
1 teaspoon dried thyme
Salt and black pepper, to taste
Grated Parmesan cheese, for serving (optional)

Instructions:

In a large soup pot or Dutch oven, heat the olive oil and butter over medium heat. Add the chopped onion, diced carrots, and diced celery. Sauté for a few minutes until the vegetables become tender and the onion turns translucent.

Add the minced garlic to the pot and cook for another minute until fragrant.

Pour in the chicken broth and bring it to a simmer. Add the shredded cooked chicken to the simmering broth and let it heat through.

Stir in the half-and-half or heavy cream, and dried thyme. Season with salt and black pepper to taste. Let the soup simmer gently for a few minutes to allow the flavors to meld.

Add the gnocchi to the soup and cook according to the package instructions or until the gnocchi float to the surface, which usually takes about 2-3 minutes for store-bought gnocchi.

Once the gnocchi is cooked, stir in the fresh baby spinach and let it wilt in the hot soup.

Taste the soup and adjust the seasoning if needed.

Ladle the Chicken Gnocchi Soup into serving bowls. If desired, sprinkle grated Parmesan cheese and chopped fresh parsley over each serving for added flavor and presentation.

Enjoy this Chicken Gnocchi Soup as a hearty and comforting meal that's sure to please your taste buds and warm your soul. The combination of tender chicken, soft gnocchi, and creamy broth creates a delightful and satisfying soup that's perfect for any occasion. Buon appetito!

Minestrone Soup

Minestrone Soup is a classic Italian vegetable soup known for its hearty and wholesome flavors. It's a versatile and nutritious dish that typically includes a variety of vegetables, beans, pasta, and sometimes meat. Here's how to make this delicious and comforting Minestrone Soup:

Ingredients:

2 tablespoons olive oil
1 medium onion, chopped
2 cloves garlic, minced
2 medium carrots, diced
2 celery stalks, diced
1 zucchini, diced
1 cup green beans, trimmed and cut into bite-sized pieces
1 can (14 oz) diced tomatoes
6 cups vegetable or chicken broth (low-sodium, if possible)
1 can (14 oz) kidney beans or cannellini beans, drained and rinsed
1 cup small pasta (such as macaroni, small shells, or ditalini)
1 teaspoon dried oregano
1 teaspoon dried basil
Salt and black pepper, to taste
Grated Parmesan cheese, for serving (optional)

Instructions:

In a large soup pot or Dutch oven, heat the olive oil over medium heat. Add the chopped onion, minced garlic, diced carrots, and diced celery. Sauté for a few minutes until the vegetables become tender and the onion turns translucent.

Stir in the diced zucchini and green beans. Cook for another few minutes until the vegetables start to soften.

Pour in the diced tomatoes with their juices and the vegetable or chicken broth. Bring the soup to a simmer.

Add the drained and rinsed kidney beans or cannellini beans to the pot. Stir in the dried oregano and basil. Season with salt and black pepper to taste.

Let the Minestrone Soup simmer gently for about 15-20 minutes to allow the flavors to meld and the vegetables to cook through.

In a separate pot, cook the small pasta according to the package instructions until al dente. Drain the pasta and set aside.

Once the soup is ready, add the cooked pasta to the pot. Stir well to incorporate the pasta into the soup. Taste the Minestrone Soup and adjust the seasoning if needed.

Ladle the soup into serving bowls. If desired, sprinkle grated Parmesan cheese and chopped fresh basil over each serving for added flavor and presentation.

Enjoy this Minestrone Soup as a hearty and wholesome meal that's packed with a variety of nutritious vegetables and beans. It's a comforting and satisfying soup that's perfect for any time of the year. Serve it with some crusty bread for a complete and delicious Italian-inspired meal. Buon appetito!

Pasta e Fagioli

Pasta e Fagioli, also known as Pasta and Beans, is a classic Italian soup that is both hearty and comforting. It features a rich and flavorful broth filled with pasta, beans, vegetables, and often some pancetta or bacon for added depth of flavor. Here's how to make this delicious Pasta e Fagioli soup:

Ingredients:

2 tablespoons olive oil
1 small onion, finely chopped
2 cloves garlic, minced
2 carrots, diced
2 celery stalks, diced
4 ounces pancetta or bacon, diced (optional)
1 can (14 oz) diced tomatoes
1 can (14 oz) cannellini beans, drained and rinsed
6 cups chicken or vegetable broth (low-sodium, if possible)
1 teaspoon dried oregano
1 teaspoon dried thyme
1 bay leaf
Salt and black pepper, to taste
1 cup small pasta (such as ditalini, small shells, or elbow macaroni)
Fresh parsley, chopped, for garnish (optional)
Grated Parmesan cheese, for serving (optional)

Instructions:

In a large soup pot or Dutch oven, heat the olive oil over medium heat. Add the chopped onion, minced garlic, diced carrots, and diced celery. If using, add the diced pancetta or bacon. Sauté for a few minutes until the vegetables become tender and the onion turns translucent.

Stir in the diced tomatoes with their juices and the drained and rinsed cannellini beans. Cook for a few minutes to allow the flavors to meld.

Pour in the chicken or vegetable broth and add the dried oregano, dried thyme, and bay leaf. Season with salt and black pepper to taste.

Bring the soup to a simmer and let it cook for about 15-20 minutes to allow the flavors to develop.

In a separate pot, cook the small pasta according to the package instructions until al dente. Drain the pasta and set aside.

Once the soup is ready, add the cooked pasta to the pot. Stir well to incorporate the pasta into the soup.

Taste the Pasta e Fagioli and adjust the seasoning if needed.

Ladle the soup into serving bowls. If desired, sprinkle chopped fresh parsley and grated Parmesan cheese over each serving for added flavor and presentation.

Enjoy this Pasta e Fagioli soup as a comforting and delicious Italian-inspired meal. The combination of pasta, beans, and vegetables in a flavorful broth makes it a hearty and satisfying option for any time of the year. Serve it with some crusty bread for a complete and satisfying meal. Buon appetito!

Italian Vegetable Soup

Italian Vegetable Soup is a delicious and nutritious soup that showcases a medley of fresh vegetables, aromatic herbs, and a flavorful broth. This hearty and comforting soup is perfect for showcasing the bountiful flavors of Italian cuisine. Here's how to make this delightful Italian Vegetable Soup:

Ingredients:

2 tablespoons olive oil

1 medium onion, chopped

2 cloves garlic, minced

2 carrots, diced

2 celery stalks, diced

1 zucchini, diced

1 yellow squash, diced

1 cup green beans, trimmed and cut into bite-sized pieces

1 can (14 oz) diced tomatoes

6 cups vegetable or chicken broth (low-sodium, if possible)

1 teaspoon dried oregano

1 teaspoon dried basil

1 bay leaf

Salt and black pepper, to taste

1 cup small pasta (such as ditalini, small shells, or elbow macaroni)

Fresh parsley, chopped, for garnish (optional)

Grated Parmesan cheese, for serving (optional)

Instructions:

In a large soup pot or Dutch oven, heat the olive oil over medium heat. Add the chopped onion and minced garlic. Sauté for a few minutes until the onion becomes translucent and the garlic is fragrant.

Stir in the diced carrots, diced celery, diced zucchini, diced yellow squash, and cut green beans. Cook the vegetables for a few minutes until they start to soften.

Pour in the diced tomatoes with their juices and the vegetable or chicken broth. Add the dried oregano, dried basil, and bay leaf. Season with salt and black pepper to taste.

Bring the soup to a simmer and let it cook for about 15-20 minutes to allow the flavors to meld and the vegetables to become tender.

In a separate pot, cook the small pasta according to the package instructions until al dente. Drain the pasta and set aside.

Once the soup is ready, add the cooked pasta to the pot. Stir well to incorporate the pasta into the soup.

Taste the Italian Vegetable Soup and adjust the seasoning if needed.

Ladle the soup into serving bowls. If desired, sprinkle chopped fresh parsley and grated Parmesan cheese over each serving for added flavor and presentation.

Enjoy this Italian Vegetable Soup as a wholesome and delicious meal that celebrates the vibrant and comforting flavors of Italian cuisine. It's a perfect way to enjoy the bounty of fresh vegetables in a warm and satisfying bowl of soup. Serve it with some crusty bread or a side salad for a complete and satisfying meal. Buon appetito!

Summer Farro Salad

Summer Farro Salad is a refreshing and hearty salad that celebrates the flavors of the season. It features nutty and chewy farro, vibrant summer vegetables, and a zesty dressing that brings it all together. This salad is perfect for picnics, barbecues, or as a light and nutritious meal on its own. Here's how to make this delicious Summer Farro Salad:

Ingredients:

1 cup farro
2 cups water or vegetable broth
1 cup cherry tomatoes, halved
1 cucumber, diced
1 bell pepper (red, yellow, or orange), diced
1/4 red onion, thinly sliced
1/2 cup Kalamata olives, pitted and halved
1/4 cup fresh parsley, chopped
1/4 cup fresh basil, chopped
1/4 cup crumbled feta cheese (optional, omit for a vegan version)

For the Dressing:

3 tablespoons extra-virgin olive oil
2 tablespoons balsamic vinegar
1 clove garlic, minced
1 teaspoon Dijon mustard
Salt and black pepper, to taste

Instructions:

Rinse the farro under cold water. In a medium saucepan, combine the rinsed farro and water or vegetable broth. Bring it to a boil, then reduce the heat to low, cover, and let it simmer for about 20-25 minutes, or until the farro is tender but still slightly chewy. Drain any excess water and let the farro cool.

In a large mixing bowl, combine the cooked and cooled farro with the cherry tomatoes, cucumber, bell pepper, red onion, Kalamata olives, fresh parsley, and fresh basil.

In a separate small bowl, whisk together the extra-virgin olive oil, balsamic vinegar, minced garlic, Dijon mustard, salt, and black pepper to make the dressing.

Pour the dressing over the farro salad and toss everything together until well combined and evenly coated with the dressing.

If using, sprinkle the crumbled feta cheese over the salad for an added burst of flavor.

Chill the Summer Farro Salad in the refrigerator for at least 30 minutes to allow the flavors to meld.

Before serving, give the salad a final toss and adjust the seasoning if needed.

Enjoy this Summer Farro Salad as a delicious and nutritious dish that's perfect for warm days and gatherings. The combination of chewy farro, fresh summer vegetables, and zesty dressing makes it a satisfying and flavorful addition to any summer meal. It can be served as a side dish or as a light and filling main course. Buon appetito!

Shaved Raw Asparagus with Parmesan Dressing

Shaved Raw Asparagus with Parmesan Dressing is a delightful and elegant salad that highlights the freshness and crunch of raw asparagus. This simple yet flavorful dish is perfect for spring and summer, and it's a great way to enjoy asparagus in its raw form. Here's how to make this delicious salad:

Ingredients:

1 bunch of fresh asparagus
1/4 cup grated Parmesan cheese
2 tablespoons lemon juice
1 tablespoon Dijon mustard
1/4 cup extra-virgin olive oil
Salt and black pepper, to taste
Fresh basil leaves, chopped, for garnish (optional)

Instructions:

Wash the asparagus thoroughly and trim off the tough ends. Using a vegetable peeler or a sharp knife, carefully shave the asparagus into thin ribbons. You can also use a mandoline slicer for this step.

In a small bowl, whisk together the grated Parmesan cheese, lemon juice, and Dijon mustard until well combined.

Slowly drizzle the extra-virgin olive oil into the bowl while whisking continuously, until the dressing is emulsified and smooth. Season with salt and black pepper to taste.

In a large mixing bowl, toss the shaved asparagus ribbons with the Parmesan dressing until evenly coated.

Transfer the dressed asparagus to a serving platter or individual salad plates.

If desired, sprinkle chopped fresh basil over the salad for added flavor and presentation.

Enjoy this Shaved Raw Asparagus with Parmesan Dressing as a light and refreshing salad that celebrates the natural flavors of asparagus. The combination of the crisp asparagus ribbons and the tangy Parmesan dressing makes it a delightful side dish or a starter for any meal. It's perfect for a quick and elegant appetizer or a healthy addition to your dinner spread. Buon appetito!

Crunchy Vegetable Salad with Ricotta Crostini

Crunchy Vegetable Salad with Ricotta Crostini is a delicious and refreshing salad that features a medley of crisp and colorful vegetables, paired with creamy ricotta cheese crostini for added texture and flavor. This salad is perfect for a light and nutritious lunch or as a refreshing appetizer for a summer gathering. Here's how to make this delightful Crunchy Vegetable Salad with Ricotta Crostini:

Ingredients:

For the Salad:

2 cups mixed salad greens (such as lettuce, arugula, or spinach)
1 cup cherry tomatoes, halved
1 cucumber, thinly sliced
1 bell pepper (red, yellow, or orange), thinly sliced
1 carrot, julienned or grated
1/4 red onion, thinly sliced
1/4 cup sliced radishes
1/4 cup toasted sliced almonds
Fresh basil leaves, torn, for garnish (optional)

For the Ricotta Crostini:

Baguette or crusty bread, sliced
1 cup ricotta cheese
1 tablespoon lemon zest
1 tablespoon lemon juice
Salt and black pepper, to taste

Instructions:

In a large salad bowl, combine the mixed salad greens, halved cherry tomatoes, sliced cucumber, sliced bell pepper, julienned or grated carrot, thinly sliced red onion, and sliced radishes.
In a small bowl, whisk together the lemon zest, lemon juice, salt, and black pepper. Drizzle the dressing over the salad and toss everything together until the vegetables are evenly coated.
To make the Ricotta Crostini, toast the slices of baguette or crusty bread until they are lightly browned and crispy.
In a separate bowl, mix the ricotta cheese with a pinch of salt and black pepper. Spread a generous layer of the seasoned ricotta cheese on each toasted bread slice.
Arrange the Ricotta Crostini on a serving platter.
Sprinkle the toasted sliced almonds over the salad for added crunch and texture.
If desired, garnish the salad with torn fresh basil leaves for a burst of flavor and color.
Serve the Crunchy Vegetable Salad with Ricotta Crostini as a refreshing and vibrant dish that's sure to impress. The combination of crisp vegetables, creamy ricotta cheese crostini, and the zesty lemon dressing makes it a delightful and satisfying meal. It's a perfect option for a light lunch or as an appetizer for any occasion. Enjoy the flavors and textures of this delicious salad!
Buon appetito!

Tomato, Haricots Verts, and Potato Salad

Tomato, Haricots Verts, and Potato Salad is a delightful and nutritious salad that showcases the flavors of fresh tomatoes, tender haricots verts (French green beans), and creamy potatoes. This salad is perfect for summer picnics, barbecues, or as a light and satisfying side dish for any meal. Here's how to make this delicious Tomato, Haricots Verts, and Potato Salad:

Ingredients:

1 pound baby potatoes (red or Yukon Gold), washed and halved
8 ounces haricots verts (French green beans), trimmed
1 cup cherry tomatoes, halved
1/4 cup red onion, thinly sliced
2 tablespoons fresh parsley, chopped
2 tablespoons fresh basil, chopped
2 tablespoons extra-virgin olive oil
1 tablespoon white wine vinegar
1 teaspoon Dijon mustard
Salt and black pepper, to taste
Optional: crumbled feta cheese or goat cheese for added creaminess (omit for a dairy-free version)

Instructions:

In a large pot, bring salted water to a boil. Add the halved baby potatoes and cook until tender, about 10-12 minutes. Drain the potatoes and let them cool slightly.

In the same pot, bring another batch of salted water to a boil. Add the haricots verts and cook for 2-3 minutes until they are bright green and crisp-tender. Drain the green beans and immediately plunge them into a bowl of ice water to stop the cooking process. This will help retain their vibrant color and crunch.

In a large mixing bowl, combine the cooked and slightly cooled baby potatoes, blanched haricots verts, halved cherry tomatoes, thinly sliced red onion, chopped parsley, and chopped basil.

In a separate small bowl, whisk together the extra-virgin olive oil, white wine vinegar, Dijon mustard, salt, and black pepper to make the dressing.

Pour the dressing over the salad and toss everything together until well combined and evenly coated with the dressing.

If using, sprinkle crumbled feta cheese or goat cheese over the salad for added creaminess and tanginess.

Chill the Tomato, Haricots Verts, and Potato Salad in the refrigerator for at least 30 minutes to allow the flavors to meld.

Before serving, give the salad a final toss and adjust the seasoning if needed.

Enjoy this Tomato, Haricots Verts, and Potato Salad as a delicious and nutritious dish that celebrates the vibrant and fresh flavors of summer. The combination of tender potatoes, crisp haricots verts, juicy cherry tomatoes, and the zesty dressing makes it a satisfying and flavorful addition to any meal. Serve it as a side dish or enjoy it on its own for a light and refreshing lunch. Buon appetito!

Lemony Chickpea Salad

Lemony Chickpea Salad is a bright and refreshing salad that features the nutty flavor of chickpeas combined with the zesty tang of lemon and fresh herbs. This salad is not only delicious but also packed with protein and fiber from the chickpeas, making it a nutritious and satisfying dish. Here's how to make this delightful Lemony Chickpea Salad:

Ingredients:

2 cans (15 ounces each) chickpeas (garbanzo beans), drained and rinsed
1 cup cherry tomatoes, halved
1 cucumber, diced
1/4 red onion, thinly sliced
1/4 cup fresh parsley, chopped
1/4 cup fresh mint, chopped
Zest of 1 lemon
Juice of 1 lemon
3 tablespoons extra-virgin olive oil
Salt and black pepper, to taste
Optional: crumbled feta cheese or goat cheese for added creaminess (omit for a dairy-free version)

Instructions:

In a large mixing bowl, combine the drained and rinsed chickpeas with the halved cherry tomatoes, diced cucumber, thinly sliced red onion, chopped parsley, and chopped mint.
In a separate small bowl, whisk together the lemon zest, lemon juice, extra-virgin olive oil, salt, and black pepper to make the dressing.
Pour the dressing over the chickpea salad and toss everything together until well combined and evenly coated with the lemony dressing.
If using, sprinkle crumbled feta cheese or goat cheese over the salad for added creaminess and tanginess.
Chill the Lemony Chickpea Salad in the refrigerator for at least 30 minutes to allow the flavors to meld.
Before serving, give the salad a final toss and adjust the seasoning if needed.
Enjoy this Lemony Chickpea Salad as a refreshing and vibrant dish that's perfect for warm days and gatherings. The combination of nutty chickpeas, juicy cherry tomatoes, crisp cucumber, and the zesty lemon dressing makes it a delightful and satisfying meal. It's a versatile salad that can be served as a side dish, a light lunch, or a healthy snack. Serve it on its own or pair it with grilled chicken or fish for a complete and nutritious meal. Buon appetito!

Vegetarian Sides and Mains

Homemade Potato Gnocchi

Homemade Potato Gnocchi is a classic Italian pasta dish made with soft and pillowy potato dumplings. This delightful comfort food is surprisingly easy to make at home and requires only a few simple ingredients. Here's how to make this delicious Homemade Potato Gnocchi:

Ingredients:

2 pounds Russet potatoes (about 4 medium-sized potatoes)
1 1/2 cups all-purpose flour, plus extra for dusting
1 teaspoon salt
1 large egg, beaten

Instructions:

Wash the potatoes thoroughly and place them in a large pot of boiling water. Cook the potatoes until they are tender and can be easily pierced with a fork, about 20-25 minutes.

Drain the cooked potatoes and let them cool slightly. While they are still warm, peel the skin off the potatoes using a knife or your hands.

In a large mixing bowl, mash the peeled potatoes until they are smooth and free of lumps. You can also use a potato ricer or a food mill for this step, which will give you a smoother texture.

Add the beaten egg and salt to the mashed potatoes and mix well.

Gradually add the all-purpose flour to the potato mixture, kneading the dough gently until it comes together and forms a soft and slightly sticky ball. Be careful not to over-knead the dough, as this can make the gnocchi tough.

On a floured surface, divide the dough into smaller portions and roll each portion into a long rope, about 3/4 inch in diameter.

Using a sharp knife, cut the dough ropes into small pieces, about 1 inch in length. You can leave the gnocchi as is, or use a fork to create ridges on each piece to help sauce adhere better.

Bring a large pot of salted water to a boil. Add the gnocchi in batches, being careful not to overcrowd the pot, and cook them until they float to the surface, which should take about 2-3 minutes. Use a slotted spoon to remove the cooked gnocchi and transfer them to a plate.

Serve the Homemade Potato Gnocchi with your favorite sauce, such as marinara, pesto, or a creamy Alfredo sauce. You can also top them with grated Parmesan cheese and fresh herbs for added flavor.

Four-Cheese Stuffed Shells

Four-Cheese Stuffed Shells is a rich and indulgent Italian pasta dish that features jumbo pasta shells filled with a luscious blend of four cheeses and baked to perfection in a savory marinara sauce. This comforting and flavorful recipe is a favorite for pasta lovers and a delightful option for special occasions or family gatherings. Here's how to make this delicious Four-Cheese Stuffed Shells:

Ingredients:

1 box (12 ounces) jumbo pasta shells
2 cups ricotta cheese
1 cup shredded mozzarella cheese
1 cup grated Parmesan cheese
1 cup shredded provolone cheese
2 large eggs, beaten
1/4 cup fresh parsley, chopped
1/4 teaspoon ground nutmeg
Salt and black pepper, to taste
2 cups marinara sauce (homemade or store-bought)
Fresh basil leaves, for garnish (optional)

Instructions:

Preheat your oven to 375°F (190°C). Grease a large baking dish with cooking spray or olive oil and set aside.
Cook the jumbo pasta shells according to the package instructions until they are al dente. Drain the cooked shells and rinse them under cold water to stop the cooking process. Set the shells aside.
In a large mixing bowl, combine the ricotta cheese, shredded mozzarella cheese, grated Parmesan cheese, shredded provolone cheese, beaten eggs, chopped parsley, ground nutmeg, salt, and black pepper. Mix everything together until well combined and smooth.
Using a spoon, carefully stuff each cooked jumbo pasta shell with the four-cheese mixture. You can also use a piping bag or a ziplock bag with the corner snipped off for this step, which can make the filling process easier.
Arrange the stuffed shells in the prepared baking dish in a single layer.
Pour the marinara sauce evenly over the stuffed shells, making sure to cover each one with sauce.
Cover the baking dish with aluminum foil and bake in the preheated oven for about 25-30 minutes, or until the filling is heated through and the sauce is bubbly.
Remove the foil and continue baking for an additional 5-10 minutes, or until the cheese on top is melted and lightly golden.
Garnish the Four-Cheese Stuffed Shells with fresh basil leaves for added freshness and presentation.

Dreamy Polenta

Dreamy Polenta is a comforting and creamy Italian dish made from coarsely ground cornmeal. It is a versatile side dish that can be served with a variety of toppings, sauces, or as a base for other delicious dishes. Here's how to make this delightful Dreamy Polenta:

Ingredients:

1 cup coarsely ground yellow cornmeal (polenta)
4 cups water or vegetable broth
1 teaspoon salt
2 tablespoons unsalted butter (or olive oil for a dairy-free version)
1/2 cup grated Parmesan cheese (optional, omit for a dairy-free version)
Freshly ground black pepper, to taste

Instructions:

In a large saucepan, bring the water or vegetable broth to a boil over medium-high heat.
Gradually whisk in the coarsely ground cornmeal (polenta) and salt, stirring constantly to prevent lumps from forming.
Reduce the heat to low and let the polenta simmer, stirring frequently with a wooden spoon or whisk. This helps to prevent sticking and ensures even cooking.
Cook the polenta for about 20-30 minutes, or until it thickens and the grains are tender. The cooking time may vary depending on the coarseness of the cornmeal, so follow the package instructions for more precise cooking times.
Once the polenta reaches your desired consistency (smooth and creamy), remove the saucepan from the heat.
Stir in the unsalted butter (or olive oil) until it is fully incorporated, adding a richness to the polenta.
If using, stir in the grated Parmesan cheese for added creaminess and savory flavor.
Season the Dreamy Polenta with freshly ground black pepper to taste. You can also adjust the salt if needed.
Serve the polenta hot as a delicious and comforting side dish. It pairs wonderfully with grilled vegetables, sautéed mushrooms, roasted meats, or a flavorful tomato-based sauce.

Eggplant Rollatini

Eggplant Rollatini is a delicious Italian dish that features thinly sliced eggplant rolled around a flavorful filling, typically made with ricotta cheese and herbs, baked in marinara sauce, and topped with melted cheese. This dish is a wonderful combination of textures and flavors, making it a favorite among vegetarians and non-vegetarians alike. Here's how to make this delightful Eggplant Rollatini:

Ingredients:
2 medium-sized eggplants
Salt, for sweating the eggplant
Olive oil, for brushing the eggplant slices
2 cups ricotta cheese
1/2 cup grated Parmesan cheese
1 large egg
1/4 cup fresh parsley, chopped
1 teaspoon dried oregano
1 teaspoon dried basil
Salt and black pepper, to taste
2 cups marinara sauce (homemade or store-bought)
1 cup shredded mozzarella cheese

Instructions:

Preheat your oven to 375°F (190°C). Grease a large baking dish with olive oil or cooking spray and set aside.
Slice the eggplants lengthwise into approximately 1/4-inch thick slices. Sprinkle salt on both sides of the eggplant slices and let them sit for about 15-20 minutes. This process helps draw out excess moisture from the eggplant, making them less bitter and easier to roll.
After 15-20 minutes, pat the eggplant slices dry with paper towels to remove the excess salt and moisture.
Brush both sides of the eggplant slices with olive oil and arrange them in a single layer on a baking sheet. You can also grill or pan-fry the eggplant slices instead of baking them, if you prefer.
Bake the eggplant slices in the preheated oven for about 10 minutes, or until they are slightly softened and lightly browned. This step will make them pliable for rolling.
In a mixing bowl, combine the ricotta cheese, grated Parmesan cheese, egg, chopped parsley, dried oregano, dried basil, salt, and black pepper. Mix everything together until well combined.
Place a spoonful of the ricotta cheese mixture at the wider end of each eggplant slice. Roll up the slice, enclosing the filling, and place the rolled eggplant seam side down in the greased baking dish.
Pour the marinara sauce evenly over the rolled eggplant in the baking dish, making sure to cover each roll with sauce.
Sprinkle shredded mozzarella cheese over the top of the Eggplant Rollatini.
Cover the baking dish with aluminum foil and bake in the preheated oven for about 20 minutes.
Remove the foil and continue baking for an additional 10 minutes, or until the cheese is melted and bubbly and the eggplant is fully cooked.
Let the Eggplant Rollatini rest for a few minutes before serving.

Pull-Apart Herb Bread

Pull-Apart Herb Bread is a mouthwatering and savory bread dish that features soft and fluffy bread rolls infused with aromatic herbs and garlic. This delightful bread is perfect for sharing with friends and family as you can easily pull apart the rolls to enjoy their delicious flavors. Here's how to make this tasty Pull-Apart Herb Bread:

Ingredients:

For the dough:

3 cups all-purpose flour
2 1/4 teaspoons active dry yeast (1 packet)
1 cup warm milk (around 110°F or 45°C)
3 tablespoons unsalted butter, melted
1 tablespoon granulated sugar
1 teaspoon salt

For the herb butter:

1/4 cup unsalted butter, softened
2 garlic cloves, minced
1 tablespoon fresh parsley, chopped
1 tablespoon fresh basil, chopped
1 tablespoon fresh thyme leaves
1/2 teaspoon dried oregano
1/4 teaspoon salt
A pinch of black pepper

Instructions:
In a small bowl, mix warm milk with sugar and yeast. Let it sit for about 5 minutes until the yeast becomes frothy.
In a large mixing bowl, combine the all-purpose flour and salt. Add the melted butter and the activated yeast mixture to the flour. Mix everything together until a soft dough forms.
Transfer the dough to a floured surface and knead it for about 5-7 minutes until it becomes smooth and elastic. You can also use a stand mixer with a dough hook attachment for this step.
Place the dough in a greased bowl, cover it with a damp kitchen towel, and let it rise in a warm, draft-free place for about 1-1.5 hours, or until it doubles in size.
While the dough is rising, prepare the herb butter. In a small bowl, mix the softened butter with minced garlic, chopped parsley, basil, thyme, oregano, salt, and black pepper. Set aside.
Once the dough has risen, punch it down to release the air. Divide the dough into small equal-sized pieces and roll them into balls.
Take each dough ball and flatten it into a small disk. Place a small dollop of the herb butter in the center of the disk.
Carefully seal the dough around the herb butter, ensuring it is completely enclosed. Roll it gently in your palms to form a smooth ball.
Grease a 9x5-inch loaf pan or a baking dish of your choice. Arrange the filled dough balls in the pan, leaving a little space between them.
Cover the pan with a damp kitchen towel and let the dough balls rise for an additional 30-45 minutes, or until they puff up.
Preheat your oven to 375°F (190°C).
Once the dough balls have risen, bake the Pull-Apart Herb Bread in the preheated oven for 25-30 minutes, or until the top turns golden brown.
Remove the bread from the oven and brush the top with any remaining herb butter for added flavor and shine.
Let the bread cool slightly before serving. To enjoy, pull apart the soft bread rolls to reveal the herby goodness inside.
\Serve the Pull-Apart Herb Bread as a delightful appetizer or side dish with your favorite dips, soups, or salads. The combination of soft bread and aromatic herbs makes this bread a crowd-pleaser and a great addition to any meal. Enjoy the delightful flavors and the fun of pulling apart these delicious bread rolls with your loved ones. Buon appetito!

Poultry And Meat Mains

Italian Stuffed Peppers (with Sausage)

Italian Stuffed Peppers with Sausage is a delicious and hearty Italian-inspired dish that features bell peppers filled with a flavorful mixture of sausage, rice, tomatoes, herbs, and cheese. These stuffed peppers are baked to perfection, creating a satisfying and comforting meal that the whole family will love. Here's how to make this delightful Italian Stuffed Peppers with Sausage:

Ingredients:

4 large bell peppers (any color), halved and seeds removed
1 pound Italian sausage (mild or hot), casings removed
1 cup cooked rice (white or brown)
1 cup diced tomatoes (canned or fresh)
1/2 cup shredded mozzarella cheese
1/4 cup grated Parmesan cheese
1 small onion, finely chopped
2 garlic cloves, minced
2 tablespoons olive oil
1 teaspoon dried basil
1 teaspoon dried oregano
Salt and black pepper, to taste
Fresh parsley, for garnish (optional)

Instructions:

Preheat your oven to 375°F (190°C).

In a large skillet, heat the olive oil over medium heat. Add the chopped onion and garlic, and sauté until softened and fragrant.

Add the Italian sausage to the skillet and cook, breaking it up with a wooden spoon, until browned and fully cooked. Drain any excess fat if needed.

Stir in the cooked rice, diced tomatoes, dried basil, dried oregano, salt, and black pepper. Cook for a few more minutes, allowing the flavors to meld together.

Remove the skillet from the heat and stir in half of the shredded mozzarella cheese and half of the grated Parmesan cheese. Mix until the cheese is well combined with the sausage mixture.

Stuff each halved bell pepper with the sausage and rice mixture, pressing it gently to fill the cavity.

Place the stuffed peppers in a baking dish. If needed, you can add a little water to the bottom of the dish to prevent the peppers from sticking.

Sprinkle the remaining shredded mozzarella and grated Parmesan cheese over the top of the stuffed peppers.

Cover the baking dish with aluminum foil and bake in the preheated oven for 20-25 minutes, or until the peppers are tender.

Remove the foil and continue baking for an additional 5-10 minutes, or until the cheese on top is melted and lightly golden.

Garnish the Italian Stuffed Peppers with Sausage with fresh parsley, if desired.

Serve the Italian Stuffed Peppers with Sausage as a hearty and flavorful meal that's perfect for dinner. The combination of savory sausage, rice, tomatoes, and cheese inside the tender bell peppers creates a delicious harmony of tastes and textures.

These stuffed peppers can be served on their own or accompanied by a fresh salad or garlic bread for a complete and satisfying Italian-inspired meal. Enjoy this comforting dish with your loved ones and savor the deliciousness of these stuffed peppers! Buon appetito!

Italian Meatballs in Tomato Sauce

Italian Meatballs in Tomato Sauce is a classic and delicious dish that is loved by many. Here's a simple recipe to make this savory dish:

Ingredients:

For the Meatballs:

1 pound (450g) ground beef (you can also use a combination of beef and pork)
1/2 cup breadcrumbs
1/4 cup grated Parmesan cheese
1/4 cup chopped fresh parsley
1/4 cup milk
1 large egg
2 cloves garlic, minced
1 teaspoon dried oregano
1/2 teaspoon dried basil
Salt and pepper to taste

For the Tomato Sauce:

1 tablespoon olive oil
1 onion, finely chopped
2 cloves garlic, minced
1 can (28 ounces) crushed tomatoes
1 can (14 ounces) diced tomatoes
1 teaspoon dried basil
1 teaspoon dried oregano
Salt and pepper to taste
Pinch of sugar (optional, to balance the acidity of the tomatoes)

Instructions:

Preheat your oven to 400°F (200°C).

In a large mixing bowl, combine all the meatball ingredients: ground beef, breadcrumbs, grated Parmesan cheese, chopped parsley, milk, egg, minced garlic, dried oregano, dried basil, salt, and pepper. Mix everything together until well combined.

Shape the mixture into meatballs, approximately 1 to 1.5 inches in diameter, and place them on a baking sheet lined with parchment paper or lightly greased.

Bake the meatballs in the preheated oven for about 15-20 minutes or until they are cooked through and browned on the outside.

While the meatballs are baking, you can start making the tomato sauce. In a large skillet or saucepan, heat the olive oil over medium heat. Add the finely chopped onion and minced garlic and sauté until softened and translucent.

Add the crushed tomatoes and diced tomatoes to the skillet, along with the dried basil, dried oregano, salt, and pepper. If the tomatoes are too acidic, you can add a pinch of sugar to balance the flavors. Stir everything together and let the sauce simmer on low heat for about 10-15 minutes.

Once the meatballs are done baking, add them to the tomato sauce and simmer for an additional 5 minutes, allowing the flavors to meld together.

Serve the Italian Meatballs in Tomato Sauce over cooked spaghetti or your favorite pasta. You can also sprinkle some additional grated Parmesan cheese and fresh parsley on top for added flavor and presentation.

Enjoy your delicious Italian Meatballs in Tomato Sauce! Buon appetito!

Steak Pizzaiola

Steak Pizzaiola is a traditional Italian-American dish that features tender steak cooked in a flavorful tomato sauce with peppers and onions. It's a delicious and comforting meal that pairs well with pasta, rice, or crusty bread. Here's a simple recipe to make Steak Pizzaiola:

Ingredients:

2 pounds (900g) boneless beef steak (e.g., flank steak, sirloin, or ribeye), about 1-inch thick
Salt and pepper, to taste
1/4 cup all-purpose flour, for dredging
2 tablespoons olive oil
1 large onion, thinly sliced
1 bell pepper (any color), thinly sliced
3 cloves garlic, minced
1 can (28 ounces) crushed tomatoes
1 teaspoon dried oregano
1 teaspoon dried basil
1/2 teaspoon red pepper flakes (optional, for a spicy kick)
1/4 cup red wine (optional)
Fresh basil leaves, chopped, for garnish
Grated Parmesan cheese, for serving (optional)

Instructions:

Start by preparing the steak. Season both sides of the steak with salt and pepper. Then, lightly dredge the steak in flour, shaking off any excess.
In a large skillet or sauté pan, heat the olive oil over medium-high heat. Once the oil is hot, add the steak and sear it on both sides until it develops a nice golden-brown crust. This should take about 2-3 minutes per side. Once seared, remove the steak from the pan and set it aside.
In the same pan, add the sliced onion and bell pepper. Sauté them for about 5 minutes or until they become tender and slightly caramelized. Add the minced garlic and cook for an additional 1-2 minutes until fragrant.
Pour in the crushed tomatoes and add the dried oregano, dried basil, and red pepper flakes (if using). Stir everything together and let the sauce simmer on low heat for about 10 minutes to allow the flavors to meld.
If desired, you can add the red wine to the sauce and let it simmer for a few more minutes to enhance the flavors further.
Return the seared steak to the pan, making sure to coat it with the tomato sauce. Cover the pan and let the steak cook in the sauce for about 10-15 minutes or until the steak is cooked to your desired level of doneness. The cooking time will depend on the thickness of the steak and your preferred level of doneness.
Once the steak is cooked, remove it from the pan and let it rest for a few minutes before slicing.
To serve, spoon some of the tomato sauce with the peppers and onions over the sliced steak. Garnish with chopped fresh basil and, if desired, sprinkle some grated Parmesan cheese on top.
Steak Pizzaiola goes wonderfully with pasta, rice, or even a side of garlic bread. Enjoy this flavorful Italian-American dish with your favorite accompaniment! Buon appetito!

Beef Braciole

Ingredients:

For the Braciole:

4 thin slices of beef (about 1/4 inch thick and 4-6 inches wide)
Salt and pepper, to taste
1/2 cup breadcrumbs
1/4 cup grated Parmesan cheese
4 slices prosciutto or ham
4 cloves garlic, minced
1/4 cup fresh parsley, chopped
1/4 cup pine nuts (optional)
1/4 cup raisins (optional)
Kitchen twine or toothpicks for securing

For the Sauce:

2 tablespoons olive oil
1 onion, finely chopped
2 cloves garlic, minced
1 can (28 ounces) crushed tomatoes
1/2 cup red wine
1 teaspoon dried oregano
1 teaspoon dried basil
Salt and pepper, to taste

Instructions:

Prepare the Filling:
In a bowl, combine breadcrumbs, grated Parmesan cheese, minced garlic, chopped parsley, pine nuts (if using), and raisins (if using).
Mix well to create a stuffing mixture.

Assemble the Braciole:
Lay the beef slices flat on a work surface.
Season both sides of each beef slice with salt and pepper.
Place a slice of prosciutto or ham on top of each beef slice.
Divide the stuffing mixture among the beef slices, spreading it evenly over the prosciutto.

Roll and Secure:
Roll up each beef slice tightly, enclosing the stuffing.
Secure the rolls with kitchen twine or toothpicks, ensuring they hold their shape.

Prepare the Sauce:
In a large skillet or Dutch oven, heat olive oil over medium heat.
Add chopped onion and sauté until softened and translucent.
Add minced garlic and cook for another 1-2 minutes until fragrant.
Pour in the crushed tomatoes and red wine, and add dried oregano and basil.
Season with salt and pepper to taste.
Bring the sauce to a simmer and let it cook for about 10-15 minutes, allowing the flavors to meld.

Cook the Braciole:
Gently add the rolled braciole to the simmering sauce.
Cover the skillet or Dutch oven and let the braciole cook in the sauce for about 1.5 to 2 hours, or until the meat is tender and the flavors have melded.

Serve:
Once the braciole is cooked, remove the kitchen twine or toothpicks.
Serve the braciole slices with the tomato sauce spooned over them.
You can serve the beef braciole over pasta, polenta, or with crusty bread.
Enjoy your delicious homemade Beef Braciole!

Pizza

Best Margherita Pizza

For the Tomato Sauce:

1 can (14 ounces) whole peeled tomatoes, preferably San Marzano

2 cloves garlic, minced

1 tablespoon extra-virgin olive oil

Salt and pepper, to taste

Ingredients:

For the Pizza Dough:

1 pound pizza dough (store-bought or homemade)

Flour, for dusting

For the Toppings:

8 ounces fresh mozzarella cheese, sliced

Fresh basil leaves

Extra-virgin olive oil, for drizzling

Salt and pepper, to taste

Instructions:

Preheat the Oven:
Preheat your oven to the highest temperature it can reach (usually around 500-550°F or 260-290°C).

Prepare the Tomato Sauce:
In a blender or food processor, combine the whole peeled tomatoes (with their juices), minced garlic, olive oil, salt, and pepper.

Blend until you have a smooth sauce. Taste and adjust seasonings if needed.

Roll Out the Dough:
Dust your work surface with flour and roll out the pizza dough into a round shape, about 12-14 inches in diameter.

Transfer Dough to a Baking Surface:
If using a pizza stone, sprinkle it with cornmeal or flour to prevent sticking. If using a baking sheet, lightly oil it.

Transfer the rolled-out dough to the prepared baking surface.

Assemble the Pizza:
Spread a thin layer of the tomato sauce over the dough, leaving a border around the edges for the crust.

Arrange the slices of fresh mozzarella evenly over the sauce.

Tear or scatter fresh basil leaves over the cheese.

Drizzle a little extra-virgin olive oil over the toppings.

Season with a pinch of salt and freshly ground black pepper.

Bake the Pizza:
Carefully slide the pizza onto the preheated pizza stone or place the baking sheet in the hot oven.

Bake for about 10-12 minutes, or until the crust is golden and the cheese is bubbly and slightly browned.

Finish and Serve:
Once the pizza is out of the oven, let it cool for a minute or two.

Drizzle with a bit more olive oil, if desired.

Slice the Margherita pizza and serve hot.

Enjoy your delicious homemade Margherita pizza with its classic tomato, mozzarella, and basil flavors!

Pesto Pizza

Ingredients:

For the Pizza Dough:

1 pound pizza dough (store-bought or homemade)
Flour, for dusting

For the Pesto:

2 cups fresh basil leaves, packed
1/2 cup grated Parmesan cheese
1/4 cup pine nuts or walnuts
2 cloves garlic, minced
1/2 cup extra-virgin olive oil
Salt and pepper, to taste

For the Toppings:

8 ounces fresh mozzarella cheese, sliced
1 cup cherry tomatoes, halved
Red pepper flakes (optional)
Extra-virgin olive oil, for drizzling
Salt and pepper, to taste

Instructions:

Preheat the Oven:
Preheat your oven to the highest temperature it can reach (usually around 500-550°F or 260-290°C).

Prepare the Pesto:
In a food processor, combine the basil, grated Parmesan cheese, pine nuts or walnuts, minced garlic, salt, and pepper.

Pulse until the ingredients are finely chopped.

While the processor is running, slowly drizzle in the olive oil until the pesto is well combined and smooth.

Taste and adjust seasonings if needed.

Roll Out the Dough:
Dust your work surface with flour and roll out the pizza dough into a round shape, about 12-14 inches in diameter.

Transfer Dough to a Baking Surface:
If using a pizza stone, sprinkle it with cornmeal or flour to prevent sticking. If using a baking sheet, lightly oil it.

Transfer the rolled-out dough to the prepared baking surface.

Spread the Pesto:
Spread a generous layer of the freshly prepared pesto evenly over the pizza dough, leaving a border around the edges for the crust.

Add Toppings:
Arrange the sliced fresh mozzarella evenly over the pesto.

Scatter the halved cherry tomatoes over the cheese.

If desired, sprinkle red pepper flakes for a hint of heat.

Bake the Pizza:
Carefully slide the pizza onto the preheated pizza stone or place the baking sheet in the hot oven.

Bake for about 10-12 minutes, or until the crust is golden and the cheese is bubbly and slightly browned.

Finish and Serve:
Once the pizza is out of the oven, let it cool for a minute or two.

Drizzle with a bit of extra-virgin olive oil.

Season with a pinch of salt and freshly ground black pepper.

Optional Garnish:
You can garnish the cooked pizza with additional fresh basil leaves before serving.

Enjoy your delightful Pesto Pizza with its aromatic basil pesto, gooey cheese, and burst of cherry tomatoes!

Perfect Neapolitan Pizza

Creating a perfect Neapolitan pizza involves a few specific techniques and high-quality ingredients. Here's a traditional Neapolitan pizza recipe for you:

Ingredients:

For the Pizza Dough:

500g (about 17.6 ounces) Tipo 00 flour (high-protein Italian flour)
325ml (about 11 ounces) lukewarm water
10g (about 0.35 ounces) salt
2g (about 0.07 ounces) active dry yeast

For the Pizza Sauce:

1 can (14 ounces) San Marzano tomatoes (or high-quality canned tomatoes)
Salt, to taste
Fresh basil leaves

For the Toppings:

Fresh mozzarella cheese (preferably buffalo mozzarella)
Fresh basil leaves
Extra-virgin olive oil

Capricciosa Pizza

For the Toppings:

1/2 cup tomato sauce or pizza sauce
1 1/2 cups shredded mozzarella cheese
1/2 cup cooked ham, sliced
1/2 cup sliced mushrooms (sautéed or canned)
1/4 cup artichoke hearts, drained and quartered
1/4 cup pitted black olives, sliced
Salt and pepper, to taste
Fresh basil leaves (optional)

Ingredients:

For the Pizza Dough:

2 1/4 teaspoons (1 packet) active dry yeast
1 teaspoon sugar
3/4 cup warm water (110°F/43°C)
2 cups all-purpose flour
1 teaspoon salt
2 tablespoons olive oil

Instructions:

Prepare the Pizza Dough:

In a small bowl, combine the warm water, sugar, and yeast. Let it sit for about 5-10 minutes until it becomes frothy.

In a large mixing bowl, combine the flour and salt. Make a well in the center and pour in the yeast mixture and olive oil.

Mix the ingredients until a dough forms, then transfer the dough to a floured surface and knead for about 5-7 minutes until it becomes smooth and elastic.

Place the dough in a lightly oiled bowl, cover with a damp cloth, and let it rise in a warm place for about 1-2 hours, or until doubled in size.

Preheat the Oven:

Preheat your oven to the highest temperature possible, usually around 475°F (245°C) or as high as your oven goes. If you have a pizza stone, place it in the oven while preheating.

Roll Out the Dough:

Punch down the risen dough and turn it out onto a floured surface. Roll out the dough into your desired pizza shape and thickness.

Assemble the Pizza:

Transfer the rolled-out dough to a pizza peel or a baking sheet lined with parchment paper.

Spread the tomato sauce evenly over the dough, leaving a border around the edges for the crust.

Sprinkle about half of the shredded mozzarella cheese over the sauce.

Evenly distribute the sliced ham, mushrooms, artichoke hearts, and black olives over the cheese.

Sprinkle the remaining mozzarella cheese over the toppings. Season with a pinch of salt and pepper.

Bake the Pizza:

Carefully slide the pizza onto the preheated pizza stone in the oven, if using. Alternatively, bake the pizza on the baking sheet.

Bake for about 10-15 minutes or until the crust is golden brown, the cheese is melted and bubbly, and the toppings are cooked.

Finish and Serve:

Remove the pizza from the oven and let it cool slightly before slicing.

If desired, garnish with fresh basil leaves for added flavor and aroma.

Serve your homemade Capricciosa pizza hot and enjoy!

Venetian Shrimp with Polenta

Venetian Shrimp with Polenta is a delightful Italian dish that combines succulent shrimp with creamy polenta, often flavored with aromatic ingredients like garlic, white wine, and herbs. Here's a simple recipe for you to enjoy this flavorful and comforting dish:

Ingredients:

For the Shrimp:

1 pound (450g) large shrimp, peeled and deveined
2 tablespoons olive oil
3 cloves garlic, minced
1/4 teaspoon red pepper flakes (adjust to taste)
1/4 cup dry white wine
1 tablespoon fresh lemon juice
Salt and black pepper, to taste
Chopped fresh parsley, for garnish

For the Polenta:

1 cup cornmeal (polenta)
4 cups water or chicken broth
1 teaspoon salt
1/2 cup grated Parmesan cheese
2 tablespoons unsalted butter

Instructions:

For the Polenta:

In a large saucepan, bring the water or chicken broth to a boil. Add the salt.
Gradually whisk in the cornmeal, stirring constantly to avoid lumps.
Reduce the heat to low and simmer, stirring frequently, for about 20-30 minutes or until the polenta is thick and creamy.
Stir in the grated Parmesan cheese and butter until melted and well combined. Adjust the seasoning if needed. Keep warm while you prepare the shrimp.

For the Shrimp:

In a large skillet, heat the olive oil over medium heat.
Add the minced garlic and red pepper flakes. Sauté for about 1 minute until fragrant.
Add the shrimp to the skillet and cook for 2-3 minutes on each side until they turn pink and opaque.
Pour in the white wine and lemon juice. Let it simmer for another 2-3 minutes to allow the flavors to meld and the alcohol to cook off.
Season with salt and black pepper to taste. Adjust the level of spiciness by adding more red pepper flakes if desired.
Remove the skillet from heat and sprinkle chopped fresh parsley over the shrimp.

To Serve:

Spoon a generous portion of the creamy polenta onto each serving plate.
Top the polenta with the Venetian shrimp, arranging them evenly.
Drizzle some of the flavorful cooking liquid from the skillet over the shrimp and polenta.
Garnish with additional chopped parsley for a pop of color and freshness.
Serve the Venetian Shrimp with Polenta immediately as a delicious and satisfying meal.
This dish pairs well with a crisp white wine and a side salad for a complete dining experience. Enjoy the rich flavors of Venetian cuisine from the comfort of your own home!

Cioppino with Fennel and Saffron

Cioppino is a flavorful Italian-American seafood stew that originated in San Francisco. It's typically made with a variety of seafood, such as fish, shrimp, mussels, and clams, cooked in a rich tomato-based broth. Adding fennel and saffron to the Cioppino adds a unique depth of flavor and aromatic quality. Here's a recipe for Cioppino with Fennel and Saffron:

Ingredients:

1 pound mixed seafood (such as firm white fish, shrimp, mussels, and clams), cleaned and deveined
2 tablespoons olive oil
1 onion, finely chopped
1 fennel bulb, thinly sliced
3 cloves garlic, minced
1/2 teaspoon red pepper flakes (adjust to taste)
1/2 cup dry white wine
1 (28-ounce) can crushed tomatoes
4 cups fish or seafood broth
1/2 teaspoon saffron threads
1 bay leaf
Salt and black pepper, to taste
Chopped fresh parsley, for garnish
Crusty bread, for serving

Instructions:

In a small bowl, combine the saffron threads with a few tablespoons of warm water. Let it steep and release its flavor and color.
In a large pot or Dutch oven, heat the olive oil over medium heat. Add the chopped onion and sliced fennel. Sauté for about 5-7 minutes, until the vegetables are softened and translucent.
Add the minced garlic and red pepper flakes. Sauté for another minute until fragrant.
Pour in the white wine and let it simmer for a couple of minutes to reduce slightly.
Add the crushed tomatoes, fish or seafood broth, bay leaf, and the steeped saffron (along with the soaking liquid) to the pot. Stir to combine. Season with salt and black pepper to taste.
Bring the broth to a gentle simmer and let it cook for about 15-20 minutes, allowing the flavors to meld and the broth to reduce slightly.
Carefully add the mixed seafood to the pot, starting with the firmest seafood (such as fish) and gradually adding the more delicate options (like shrimp, mussels, and clams).
Cover the pot and let the seafood cook in the simmering broth for about 5-8 minutes, or until the seafood is cooked through. Discard any mussels or clams that do not open.
Taste the broth and adjust the seasoning if needed.
To serve, ladle the Cioppino into bowls. Garnish with chopped fresh parsley for a burst of freshness and color.
Serve the Cioppino with Fennel and Saffron with crusty bread on the side for dipping and soaking up the delicious broth.

Lobster Risotto

Lobster risotto is a luxurious and indulgent dish that combines the rich flavors of tender lobster meat with creamy Arborio rice cooked in a flavorful broth. Here's a recipe for lobster risotto that you can try:

Ingredients:

2 small lobster tails or 1 large lobster tail
1 cup Arborio rice
4 cups seafood or chicken broth
1/2 cup dry white wine
1/2 onion, finely chopped
2 cloves garlic, minced
2 tablespoons butter
2 tablespoons olive oil
1/4 cup grated Parmesan cheese
Salt and black pepper, to taste
Fresh parsley, chopped, for garnish

Instructions:

Prepare the Lobster:
If using whole lobster tails, use kitchen shears to carefully cut down the middle of the top shell. Gently pull apart the shell and remove the lobster meat. Cut the meat into bite-sized pieces. Keep the shells for making lobster broth (optional).

If using pre-cooked lobster meat, chop it into bite-sized pieces.

Make Lobster Broth (Optional):
If using lobster shells, place them in a pot and cover with water. Simmer for about 20-30 minutes to create a lobster broth. Strain and reserve the broth for later use.

Prepare the Risotto:
In a large skillet or sauté pan, heat the olive oil and 1 tablespoon of butter over medium heat. Add the chopped onion and sauté until translucent.

Add the minced garlic and Arborio rice. Stir to coat the rice with the butter and oil. Cook for about 1-2 minutes until the rice is lightly toasted.

Deglaze with Wine:
Pour in the dry white wine and cook until it's mostly absorbed by the rice, stirring frequently.

Add Broth:
Begin adding the seafood or chicken broth, one ladleful at a time, to the rice. Stir frequently and allow the liquid to be absorbed before adding more broth. Continue this process until the rice is creamy and cooked al dente. This will take about 18-20 minutes.

Incorporate Lobster:
When the risotto is almost cooked, add the chopped lobster meat to the pan. Stir gently to combine and warm the lobster.

Finish the Dish:
Stir in the remaining tablespoon of butter and the grated Parmesan cheese. Season with salt and black pepper to taste.

Serve:
Ladle the lobster risotto onto serving plates or bowls. Garnish with chopped fresh parsley for a burst of color and freshness.

Spaghetti with Clams and Garlic

Spaghetti with clams and garlic, also known as "Spaghetti alle Vongole" in Italian, is a classic and flavorful dish that highlights the natural sweetness of clams and the aromatic quality of garlic. Here's a simple recipe for you to enjoy this delicious pasta dish:

12 ounces (340g) spaghetti
2 dozen fresh clams, scrubbed and rinsed
4 tablespoons olive oil
4 cloves garlic, thinly sliced
1/2 teaspoon red pepper flakes (adjust to taste)
1/4 cup dry white wine
1/4 cup fresh parsley, chopped
Salt and black pepper, to taste
Lemon wedges, for serving (optional)

Instructions:

Cook the Pasta:
Bring a large pot of salted water to a boil. Add the spaghetti and cook according to the package instructions until al dente. Reserve about 1/2 cup of pasta cooking water before draining.

Prepare the Clams:
In a large skillet or sauté pan, heat 2 tablespoons of olive oil over medium heat. Add the clams and cook for a few minutes until they start to open. Discard any clams that do not open.

Sauté the Garlic:
Push the clams to the sides of the pan and add the remaining 2 tablespoons of olive oil to the center. Add the thinly sliced garlic and red pepper flakes. Sauté for about 1 minute until the garlic is fragrant and just beginning to turn golden.

Deglaze with Wine:
Pour in the dry white wine and let it simmer for a minute or two to cook off the alcohol.

Combine Pasta and Clams:
Add the cooked spaghetti to the pan with the clams and garlic. Toss everything together to coat the pasta with the flavorful sauce.

Finish the Dish:
If the pasta seems a bit dry, add some of the reserved pasta cooking water a little at a time to create a silky sauce that coats the pasta.
Stir in the chopped fresh parsley, reserving some for garnish. Season with salt and black pepper to taste.

Serve:
Divide the spaghetti with clams and garlic among serving plates. Garnish with additional chopped parsley.
Serve with lemon wedges on the side for squeezing over the dish, if desired.

Enjoy:
Enjoy your Spaghetti with Clams and Garlic immediately while it's hot. The combination of the tender clams, aromatic garlic, and perfectly cooked pasta makes for a delightful and satisfying meal.

This dish is a celebration of simple and fresh ingredients, allowing the flavors of the clams and garlic to shine. It's a wonderful option for seafood lovers and a great way to enjoy the taste of the sea in a comforting pasta dish.

Langoustines alla Busara

Langoustines alla Busara is a delicious seafood dish originating from the coastal regions of Croatia, particularly in places like Istria and Dalmatia. It features langoustines, a type of small lobster or prawn, cooked in a flavorful tomato-based sauce enriched with wine and aromatic ingredients. The result is a rich and savory dish that highlights the natural sweetness of the langoustines.

Ingredients:

1 pound (450g) langoustines, cleaned and deveined
1/4 cup olive oil
1 onion, finely chopped
2 cloves garlic, minced
1/2 teaspoon red pepper flakes (adjust to taste)
1/2 cup dry white wine
1 (14-ounce) can crushed tomatoes
1 teaspoon tomato paste (optional)
1 bay leaf
Salt and black pepper, to taste
Chopped fresh parsley, for garnish
Crusty bread, for serving

Instructions:

In a large skillet or sauté pan, heat the olive oil over medium heat.
Add the chopped onion and sauté until translucent.
Add the minced garlic and red pepper flakes. Sauté for another minute until fragrant.
Pour in the dry white wine and let it simmer for a couple of minutes to reduce slightly.
Add the crushed tomatoes, tomato paste (if using), and bay leaf to the pan. Stir to combine.
Season the sauce with salt and black pepper to taste. Let the sauce simmer for about 15-20 minutes, allowing the flavors to meld and the sauce to thicken.
Add the cleaned langoustines to the pan. Cover and cook for about 5-7 minutes, or until the langoustines turn opaque and are cooked through.
Taste the sauce and adjust the seasoning if needed.
To serve, ladle the Langoustines alla Busara onto serving plates. Garnish with chopped fresh parsley for a burst of color and freshness.
Serve the dish with crusty bread on the side for dipping and soaking up the delicious sauce.

Langoustines alla Busara is a delightful dish that captures the essence of Mediterranean flavors and seafood. It's perfect for special occasions or whenever you want to enjoy a taste of the Adriatic coast. The combination of langoustines, tomato sauce, and wine creates a harmonious and comforting dish that is sure to please seafood enthusiasts.

Thank you for choosing to embark on this culinary journey with me and for entrusting me with a small part of your kitchen adventures.

Your support and trust mean the world to me. Every recipe, every technique, and every story shared in this cookbook is a reflection of my passion for food and my desire to bring joy to your tables. Your decision to purchase this cookbook not only encourages me to continue sharing my culinary knowledge but also supports the countless hours of recipe testing, writing, and photography that went into its creation.

Wishing you many happy moments of deliciousness and culinary creativity!

For Zian And Milan, who brings smiles to my face and joy to my heart every day

www.ingramcontent.com/pod-product-compliance
Lightning Source LLC
Chambersburg PA
CBHW071319080526
44587CB00018B/3281